WONDERS
OF THE WORLD

© 2006 Brijbasi Art Press Limited
India office: A-81, Sector V, Noida, 201301
E-mail: hellofriend@brijbasiartpress.com

Written by
SHABNAM GUPTA

Edited by
KIRTI KAUL
EMAN CHOWDHARY

Art Director
SANJAY DHIMAN, PRIYABRATA ROY CHOWDHURY

Designed by
RAVINDER SINGH

Ilustrated by
ARIJIT CHOWDHURY, CHANDOO, SHIJU, ANEESH,
RAKESH GURUNG, RAJEEV, MANOJ, VIKASH,
RAJENDRA NATH AND AJAY

All rights reserved. No part of this publication may be
reproduced in any form or by means, electronic or mechanical,
including photocopy, recording or any other information
storage and retrieval system, without prior permission
in writing from the publisher.

ISBN: 81-87108-07-X

Published in 2007 by Om Books International, 4379/4B Prakash House,
Ansari Road, Darya Ganj, New Delhi 110 002, India
Tel.: 91 11 23263363/23265303. email : sales@ombooks.com

CONTENTS

ANCIENT WONDERS I   6 - 7
ANCIENT WONDERS II   8 - 9
MEDIEVAL WONDERS   10 - 11
MODERN WONDERS I   12 - 13
MODERN WONDERS II   14 - 15
LESSER KNOWN WONDERS   16 - 17
NATURAL WONDERS I   18 - 19
NATURAL WONDERS II   20 - 21
UNDERWATER WONDERS   22 - 23
DAMS AND BRIDGES   24 - 25
GRAND MONUMENTS   26 - 27
ROYAL PALACES   28 - 29
ANCIENT CITIES   30 - 31
WORLD'S TALLEST BUILDINGS   32 - 33
HOLY CITIES   34 - 35
SCULPTURES AND MEMORIALS   36 - 37
TEMPLES, MOSQUES AND CHURCHES I   38 - 39
TEMPLES, MOSQUES AND CHURCHES II   40 - 41
WORLD'S TALLEST, HIGHEST, LONGEST, LARGEST   42 - 43
DID YOU KNOW?   44 - 45
ANSWERS   46

Ancient Wonders I

Philo, an engineer living in Alexandria, Egypt, during the 2nd century BC, wrote a book called 'On the Seven Wonders'. He wrote of seven monuments that people would travel far to see and admire immensely for their craftsmanship. Today, only one of these wonders survives – the Pyramid of Giza. After a lot of research, the historians have managed to reconstruct the other wonders as well.

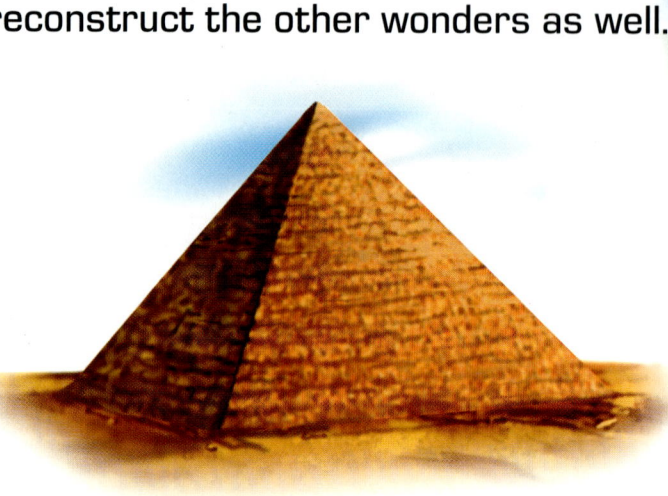

△ The Great Pyramid of Giza is 454 feet high.

⌃ The Great Pyramid of Giza, Egypt

This giant tomb was the burial place of Khufu, an Egyptian pharaoh, about 4500 years ago. It is a four-sided pyramid made entirely of stone. The pyramid was built as an almanac and can measure the length of the year. The pyramid proves the mastery that ancient Egyptians had over mathematics and astronomy.

❯ The Hanging Gardens of Babylon

The Hanging Garden was located on the East bank of River Euphrates and was built by the famous King Nebuchadnezzar II in about 605 BC. The garden was built on high terraces with green leaves and branches growing all over the walls. The garden had been built to please his Persian wife, Amytis, since she missed the greenery of her native country.

WONDERS OF THE WORLD

The Mausoleum at Halicarnassus

The Hanging Gardens of Babylon

The Pyramids of Egypt

▸ The Statue of Zeus, Olympia, Greece

The colossal statue of God Zeus, seated on a throne is approximately 40 feet tall and 20 feet wide at the base. Covered with gold and ivory, it was made by the famous Athenian sculptor, Phidias, in about 435 BC. With God Zeus' head almost touching the ceiling of the temple, you can imagine what would have happened, if Zeus would have decided to stand up!

⌃ *The throne of Zeus was decorated with gold, precious stones, ebony and ivory.*

Water from the river Tigris ▸ was pumped up to irrigate the plants and the trees at the Hanging Garden.

FUN FACTS!

Phidias used to craft his statues in his studio and later assemble them at a site. This explains why the giant statue of Zeus looked bigger than the temple in which it had been placed.

Ancient Wonders II

For years, it was the beauty of the Mausoleum rather than it's size that attracted visitors to this tomb.

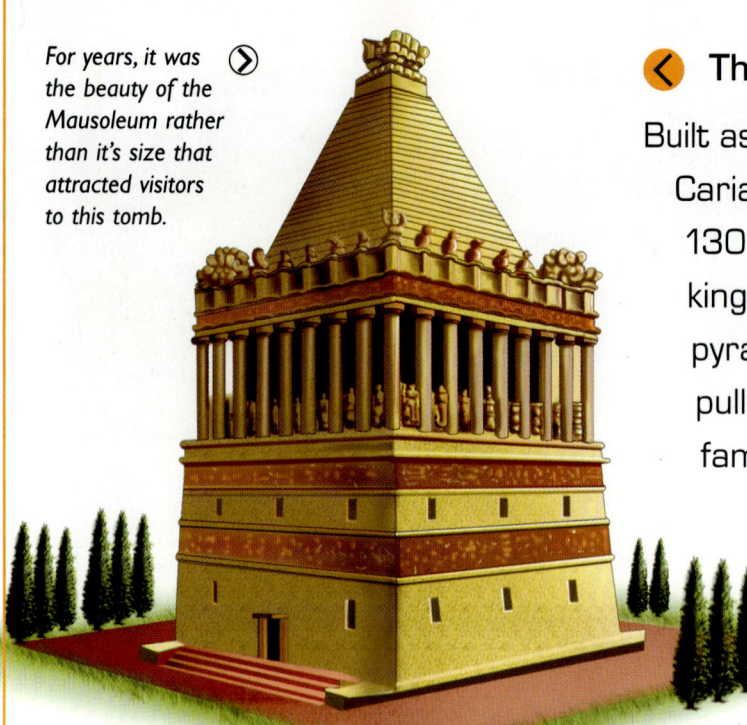

The Mausoleum at Halicarnassus, Turkey

Built as a burial monument for King Mausolus of Caria by his wife Queen Artemisia, this 130 feet high tomb had huge statues of the king and his wife. The roof was shaped like a pyramid and it had a carved chariot on top, pulled by four horses. This tomb became so famous that from then on all the large tombs are called 'mausoleums'.

With an estimated height of 383-440 feet, the Pharos of Alexandria was considered the tallest man-made structure for many centuries.

The Temple of Artemis at Ephesus, Turkey

Croesus, the King of Lydia, had a temple built in about 550 BC. Constructed at Ephesus (present day Turkey), it was built in honour of Artemis, the Greek goddess of hunting and birth. The Romans worshipped this goddess as Diana. With 106 marble columns, elaborate marble sculptures, carvings and paintings, this temple was an amazing architectural masterpiece.

The Temple of Artemis was burnt down by a man named Herostratus, in order to immortalise his name.

8-9

WONDERS OF THE WORLD

▶ The Colossus of Rhodes, Greece

Located in Greece, this was a giant 108 feet high statue of the Greek Sun god, Helios. It took about 12 years to complete and had a stone and iron framework with an outer shell of bronze. The statue collapsed in an earthquake in 226 BC, having stood for just about 20 years.

◀ The Pharos of Alexandria, Egypt

This 500 feet high lighthouse was located on the island of Pharos, at the entrance to the Alexandria harbour, Egypt. Being so huge and well lit, it was able to guide ships for long distances. This impressive wonder lasted all of 1500 years!

The fallen statue of Colossus was left untouched, until 653 AD. Raiding Arabs broke up the remains and sold the bronze for scrap.

FUN FACTS!

In ancient times, the Greek city states used to hold sporting events every four years, just like the Olympic games held today. These games were held in honour of Zeus.

Medieval Wonders

In the past, kings got the state architects and builders to design and construct some of the most wonderful buildings. However, only some of them could withstand the ravages of time. Down the years, these wonderful structures found their place in history.

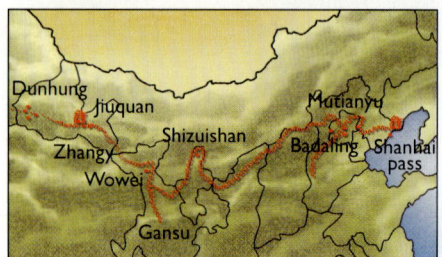

The Great Wall of China is only a few metres wide.

The Great Wall of China

Though the construction of 'The Great Wall of China' was initiated by Emperor Shi Huangdi in about 221 BC, it was the Qin dynasty (221-206 BC) that hastened the work towards its completion. The work lasted for centuries, and each successive dynasty added to the height, length and breadth of the wall. Today, with a length of over 7300 km, it is one of the longest structures ever built in the world.

The Catacombs of Kom el Shoqafa, Alexandria, Egypt

Built as burial grounds, there were a number of catacombs in Egypt. However, these lied undiscovered for many centuries. The catacomb of Kom el Shoqafa had three levels with a spiral staircase. It also had a separate area for hosting a feast in the memory of the dead. Many beautiful sculptures adorned the walls of this catacomb.

WONDERS OF THE WORLD

The Parthenon, Athens, Greece

This amazing temple, perched on the Acropolis hill, was built between 447 BC to 432 BC. It was dedicated to the city's patron-goddess, Athena Parthenos. There are eight columns at each end and 17 columns along each side. Inside the temple, there are two chambers– one for the statue of the goddess and the other for the temple treasury.

Like most Greek temples, the Parthenon was used as a treasury.

The Stonehenge complex was built almost over a period of 2,000 years.

The Stonehenge, Britian

The Stonhenge, is approximately 5000 years old! However, what we see today are the ruins of the original monument. One wonders how such big pieces of stone were carried to this place without the help of machines! The purpose of these stone pillars and ditches is not clear, though, historians claim that it could have been used as an almanac or a calendar.

FUN FACTS!
The largest stones at Stonehenge are nearly 9m high and weigh over 45 tonnes.

Modern Wonders I

With the advent of modern engineering tools, constructing buildings has become much more mechanised and faster. As a result, engineers are taking up more challenges and experimenting with unusual structures and newer building materials.

◀ World Trade Center, New York, U.S.A

A complex of seven buildings designed around a central plaza was best known for its 110 storey high, Twin Towers. Designed to be the tallest buildings in the world, tower one was completed in 1972, followed by tower two in 1973. With the highest point of these buildings being 1,368 and 1,362 feet respectively, they were the tallest in the world, before the Petronas Twin Towers took over, followed by Taipei 101. This building was, however, destroyed in a terrorist attack in 2001.

▽ *About 200,000 tons of steel was used to built the World Trade Center.*

WONDERS OF THE WORLD

The Golden Gate is the most photographed bridge in the world!

◁ The Golden Gate Bridge, U.S.A

The Golden Gate Bridge, built in 1937, links San Francisco with Marin County. It is 27 kms long, and has a six-lane road and sidewalks. The towers, on either side, hold up two steel cables from which the bridge hangs.

● The Panama Canal

This was a centuries-old dream of uniting two great oceans, the Atlantic and the Pacific, for the purpose of trade and travel. Built across the Isthmus of Panama, and completed in 1914, the canal is about 64.8 km (40 miles) long.

▷ The Eiffel Tower, Paris, France

This tower was designed by Alexandre Gustave Eiffel for the great Paris Exhibition of 1889. It is about 1000 feet tall, and has survived numerous demolition attempts and natural calamities. Now, of course, no one would even dream of suggesting its demolition, since it is such an important landmark in Paris.

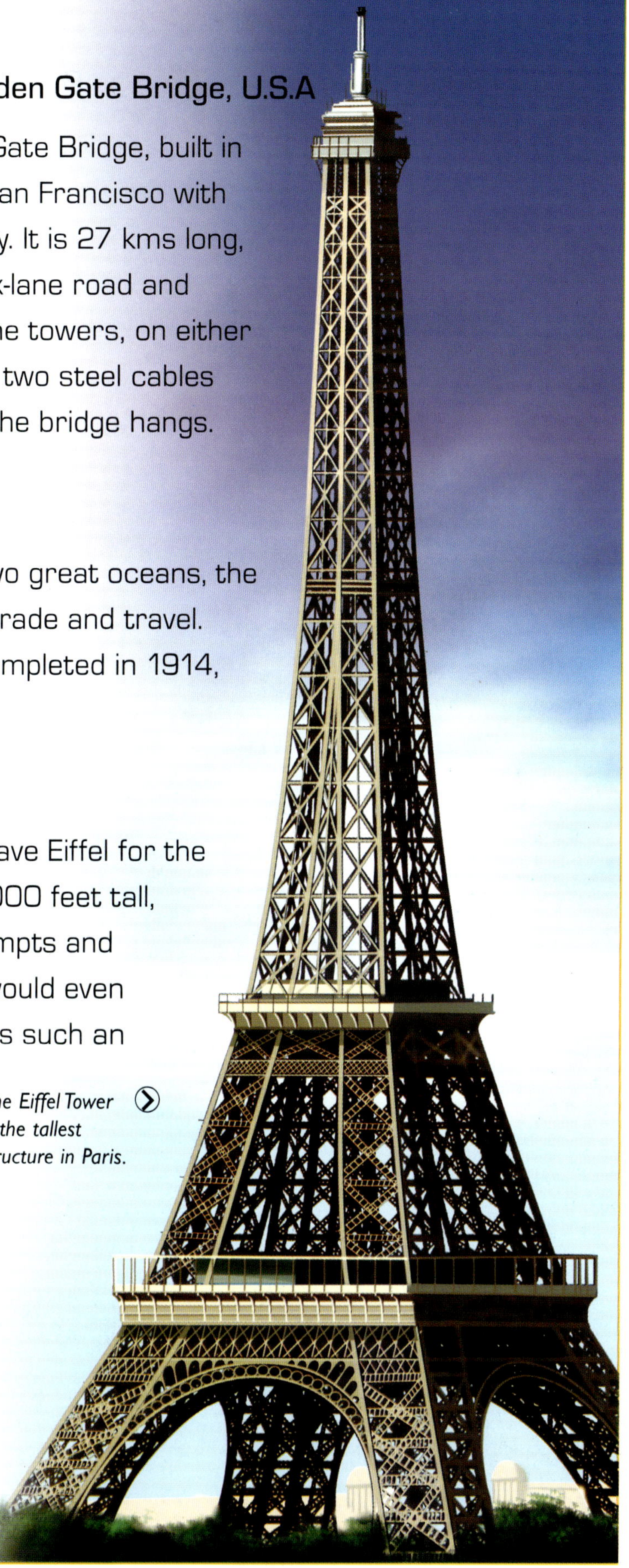

The Eiffel Tower ▷ is the tallest structure in Paris.

FUN FACTS!

Kansai International Airport, Osaka Bay, Japan, is the first offshore airport in the world. Can you imagine an airport in the sea?

Modern Wonders II

The four clocks of the Big Ben are 55 meters above the ground.

The Big Ben, London, Britain

This is the most famous clock in the world, with the biggest bell weighing 13.5 tons. The Clock Tower, which is about 320 feet high, and is also known as the 'St. Stephen's Tower', is a part of the House of Parliament. Built in 1858-59, the clock's four dials have a diameter of 23 feet each. Did you know that there is a light at the top of the tower, which when lit, indicates that the House of Commons is sitting.

Mount Rushmore is the most important tourist destination of South Dakota.

Mount Rushmore National Memorial, U.S.A

One of the world's greatest mountain carvings, Mount Rushmore is a 60-feet sculpture of the four great American presidents—George Washington, Thomas Jefferson, Theodore Roosevelt and Abraham Lincoln. A tribute to democracy, the sculptor, Gutzon Borglum, completed this masterpiece in about 14 years. Work on the carving started in 1927 and ended in 1941.

WONDERS OF THE WORLD

◀ The Hoover Dam, U.S.A

This 726 feet high dam was built across the Colorado river between 1930-36. It was named after the American President, Herbert Hoover. Hoover Dam was chosen as a National Historic Landmark in 1985.

⌃ *Hoover dam is also known as the 'Boulder Dam'.*

● Channel Tunnel

This is the world's longest undersea tunnel. Completed in 1994, the tunnel is about 50 kms long. 38 kms of the tunnel are under the English Channel, between England and France. Truly a modern engineering wonder!

▶ The CN Tower Toronto, Canada

In the late 1960's, Toronto's soaring skyline began to play havoc with signals from conventional transmission towers. To improve the situation, Canadian National Railways, or the CN, proposed building a transmission tower that would be higher than Toronto's tallest buildings. About 1,815.5 feet tall, this tower was completed in 1976.

The word CN stands for Canada's National. ▶

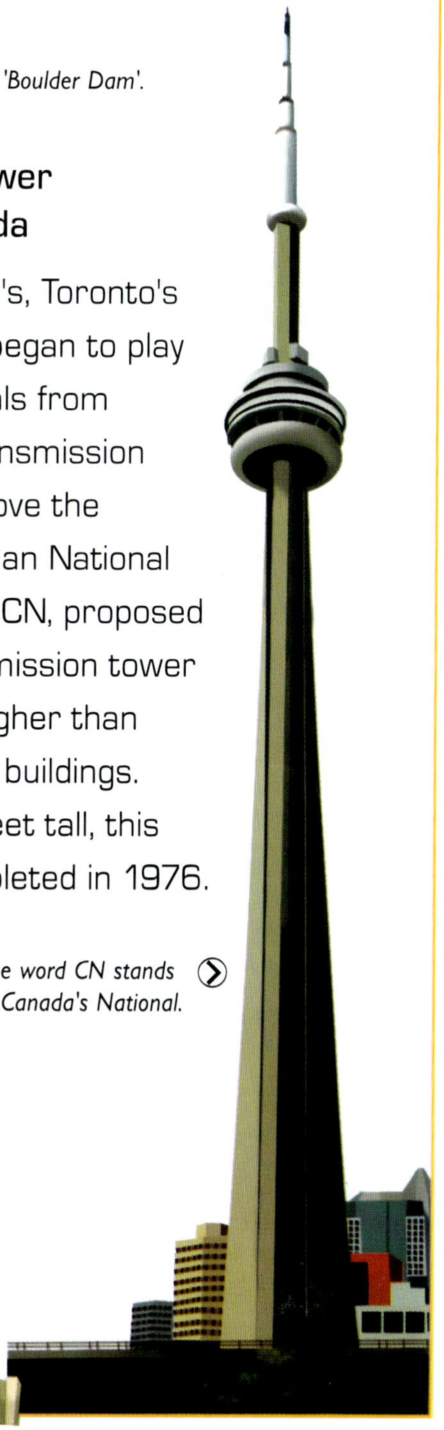

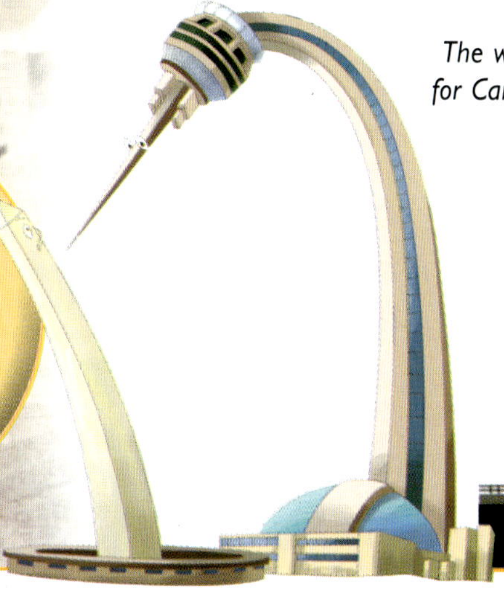

FUN FACTS!

The CN Tower is almost twice as tall as the Eiffel Tower. It is also more than three times the height of the Washington Monument.

Lesser-Known Wonders

A lot of amazing structures have been made through the ages. But, not all of them earned a place in history. Some stand forgotten, while many were lost to natural calamities. However, their ruins still speak of their past glory.

❯ The Throne Hall of Persepolis, Iran

The second largest building of the Persepolis, 'The Throne Hall' was founded in the 6th century BC by the kings of the First Persian Empire as their capital. This Throne Hall was also known as the 'Takht-e-Jamshid' or the 'Hundred Column Hall'. It had several doorways, adorned with the carvings of the king in military combat. The city of Persepolis was declared a World Heritage Site by UNESCO in 1979.

Persopolis was excavated in early 1930's.

❯ The Pyramid of the Sun, Mexico

This terraced pyramid rises over 200 feet above the city, and is considered to be the birthplace of the Sun. It was built in 2 AD along with the surrounding city of Teotihuacan and the Pyramid of the Moon. The Pyramid of the Sun is the third largest pyramid in the world.

The Pyramid of the Sun was believed to be a natural cave.

WONDERS OF THE WORLD

> ### The Petra, Jordan

Petra was famous for its many beautiful buildings and majestic rock temples. It became an important trading center around 100 AD when the Romans took over. The Deir was the largest temple in Petra. Carved from sandstone rock, it was more than 130 feet high.

Dushara was the chief god of the city of Petra.

> ### The Aztec Temple, Mexico

The Greater Temple of the Aztecs (Mexicans) is undoubtedly one of the greatest treasures lost forever. There is nothing left of the temple except for a few ruins.

It is believed that the Aztec Temple was renovated and enlarged several times.

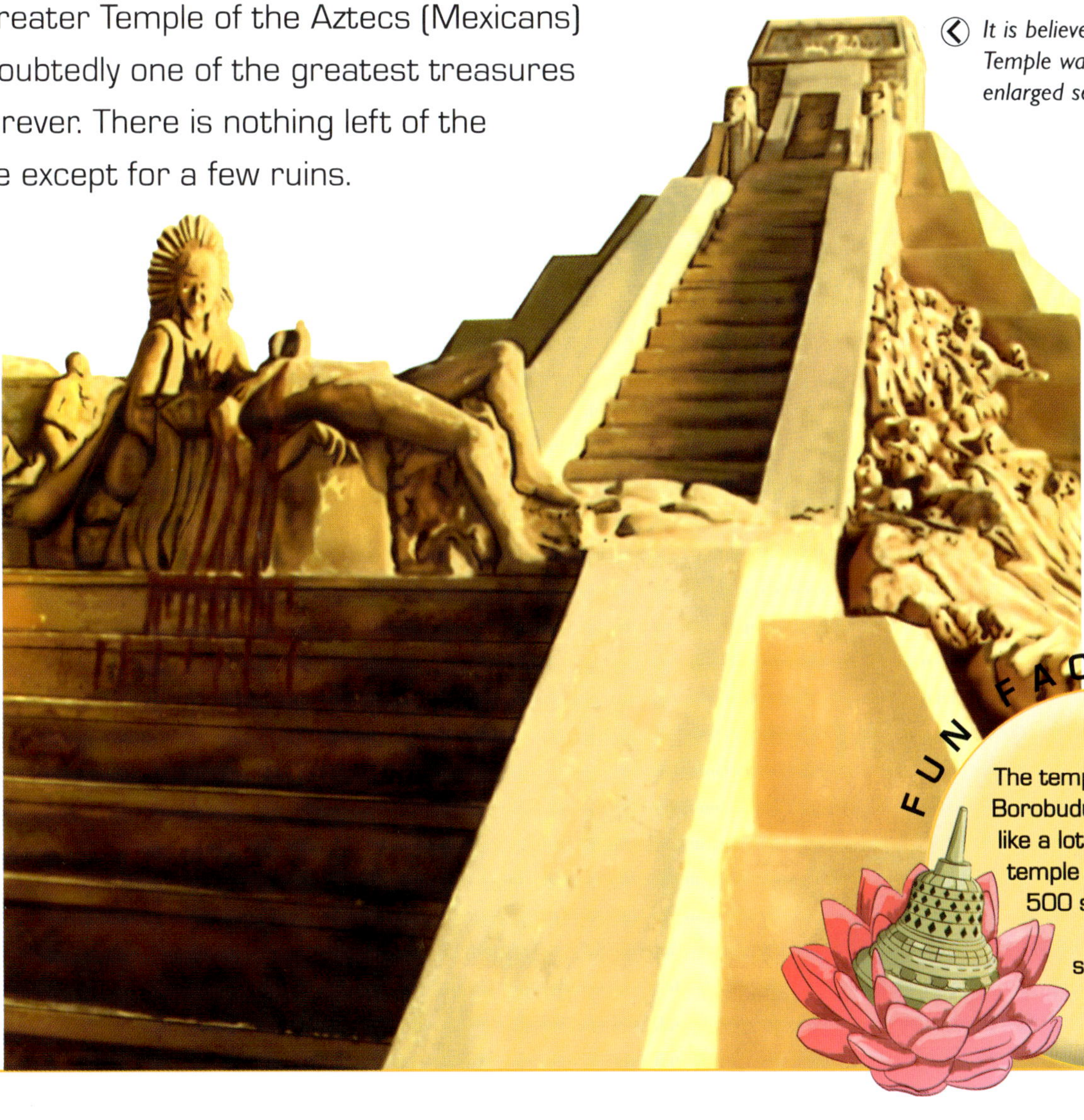

FUN FACTS!

The temple complex of Borobudur, is designed like a lotus. The entire temple has more than 500 statues of the Buddha in a sitting position.

Natural Wonders I

Pristine and beautiful, nature is a store house of amazing treasures. Snowcapped mountains, lush green forests, coral reefs, glaciers, serpentine rivers, springs, forests and several species of flora and fauna—each one of these is incredible. Some sights are even breathtaking!

❯ The Grand Canyon, U.S.A

Located in Arizona, the Grand Canyon is a steep sided gorge, carved by the fast pace of river Colarado. The pacy waters have cut through layers of rocks to transform this into a natural wonder. The canyon is nearly 0.25 to 15 miles wide and about 277 miles long.

❮ Mount Everest

Mount Everest, the highest peak of the Himalayas, is on the Nepal-Tibet border. At 29,028 feet, it is the world's highest peak. Though several attempts were made to conquer the Everest, it was only in 1953 that Edmund Hillary and Tenzing Norgay managed to summit the peak.

Mount Everest has been named after Sir George Everest, who was the first person to record it's height.

WONDERS OF THE WORLD

The Grand Canyon was first sighted in the year 1540.

● The Angel Falls, Venezuela

Falling from a height of 1000 metres, this is the highest waterfall in the world. The Angel Falls were discovered by Jimmy Angel in 1935. Angel was an American bush pilot, and the waterfall was named after him.

● The Great Barrier Reef, Australia

The Barrier Reef is the world's largest marine national park. Spread over 2000 kilometres, the reef can be seen from space. Home to about 400 varieties of corals, and thousands of plant and fish species, it is made up of millions of tiny organisms.

● The Niagara Falls

Situated on the border of Canada and U.S.A, the Niagara falls comprise of three separate waterfalls-the Horseshoe Falls, the American Falls and the smaller Bridal Veil Falls. At the highest point, these falls are almost 177 feet high. With light shining through the waters, some of the most beautiful rainbows can be seen around the Niagara Falls.

Over 20 million tourists visit the Niagara Falls every year.

FUN FACTS!
In the 19th century, stuntmen did daring feats by riding over the Niagara Falls in barrels.

Natural Wonders II

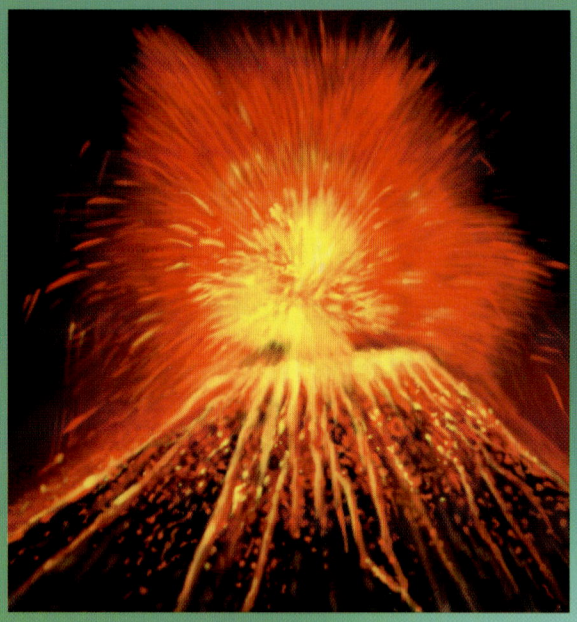

In an active state, Paricutin volcano poured out over one billion tons of lava.

Paricutin Volcano

1943 was probably the most violent year in the history of the Paricutin volcano. By the end of the year the volcano had grown 336 metres tall. For the next eight years, the volcano continued to erupt quietly and scorched an area of 25km around it. By 1952, the eruptions ended and Paricutín became dormant, reaching a height of 424 metres. The volcano has been quiet ever since.

Northern Lights

Northern lights, or the Aurora Borealis, can be seen at night in the northern latitudes. Legend has it, that these lights are a result of two mythological deities – Aurora, the Roman goddess of the dawn, and Boreas, the Greek god of the north wind, coming together. The flowing ribbons of light and wind make such lovely patterns in the night sky that people watching it swear that it is more of a supernatural, rather than a natural phenomenon.

Phang Nga Bay, Phuket, Thailand

Millions of years ago, limestone rocks were pushed up from the floor of the ocean. Over the years, these rocks were eroded by the sea waves in such a way that only the hardest amongst them were left. These rocks gradually came together and formed peaks, that were as high as 328 feet.

The cliffs of the Phang Nga Bay are streaked with hues of black, tan, ivory, gray and red..

WONDERS OF THE WORLD

From August to October, the area surrounding the Pinnacles desert blooms with wildflowers.

⌃ Pinnacles Desert, Australia

In the Pinnacles Desert, strong winds cut into the outer surface of the desert rocks, transforming them into some fantastic shapes, and even forming peaks. Some of these peaks are almost 16 feet high, making this desert, a perfect picture of raw and wild beauty.

● Torres del Paine, Chile

The mountains of Chile have slowly been worn away by the constant pressure of ice, rain and winds. This is how the Torres (or the towers) of the Torres del Paine National Park came into being. All the three summits of the Torres del Paine are well over 8530 feet high.

FUN FACTS!

A coral reef is formed when millions of tiny, colourful creatures called polyps live together. Since corals are living creatures, the Great Barrier Reef is the coral reef system structure in the whole world!

Underwater Wonders

Water can be seen in many different forms–waterfalls, lakes, seas, oceans, springs, geysers and spas. There are several spectacular sights that are found underwater. In volcanic regions, the water is usually hot. These springs or spas, have been known to have curative powers, mainly because of their mineral content.

▸ The Pammukale, Turkey

These springs have been known to have healing powers, since the second century BC. The terrace like structures, made by calcium carbonate make them look like white cotton castles.

⌄ The Galapagos Islands

The name 'Galapagos' is a Spanish word for tortoises. On this island, visitors can actually see tortoises weighing hundreds of pounds. This island group is made up of 13 major islands, eight smaller ones and 40 islets. Prisoners were exiled to these islands till 1959, after which it was declared a national park.

⌃ Pamukkale is one of the World Heritage Sites in Turkey.

The Galapagos were a favourite hideout for the pirates.

⌄ The Baikal Lake, Siberia

The Baikal is considered to be the oldest and the deepest lake in the world. More than 1,500 animal species and nearly 1,000 plant species exist in and around the lake. Baikal holds 20 percent of the Earth's fresh water, and harbours more endemic species of plants and animals than any other lake in the world.

WONDERS OF THE WORLD

The Palau Island, Pacific Ocean

This beautiful island is located in the Pacific Ocean. Marine biologists have recorded 700 species of corals, 1500 species of fish and 80 marine lakes here. Palau's coral reefs are believed to be millions of years old.

The island of Palau was discovered by the Spanish navigator, Ruy Lopez de Villalobos, in the year 1543.

The Geysir, Iceland

At Geysir, hot water spouts with such great force that it sometimes reaches a height of 200 feet! Since most of Iceland is covered by lava fields and hot springs, these hot water geysers also serve the purpose of keeping homes warm. But can you imagine how it must feel to live in a place, where the air is ice-cold and the ground warm?

It is widely believed that the Geysir began erupting in the early 14th century.

FUN FACTS!

The geyser in Yellowstone National Park, US is called 'The Old Faithful', because it spouts unfailingly every 65 minutes.

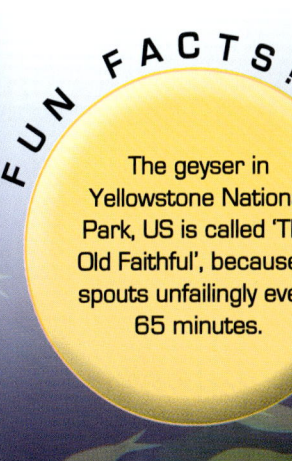

Dams and Bridges

Earth is often called the 'Blue Planet' because over two-thirds of its surface is covered with water. Though water is the source of life, too much of it can cause devastating floods. Water can be harnessed and used constructively. When held back by a dam, it can be used to produce hydroelectricity. With the advent of modern engineering tools, it has now become possible to construct dams and bridges over the most difficult water bodies.

Aswan High Dam, Egypt

This 3280 feet wide dam, built of sand and gravel was built across the river Nile in 1971. It's purpose was to hold back the water of the world's longest river. Since ancient times, the Nile has been flooding every year. This made it imperative to build a dam, so that the loss from floods could be reduced and a steady flow of water could be maintained the whole year round. Today, this dam produces more electricity than required by Egypt.

It took nearly 11 years to build the Aswan High dam.

The Tower Bridge, London, England

This bridge was built over the Thames river, London, between 1886-94. It has two towers and a drawbridge. Traffic over the bridge crosses bothways – over and under the bridge. When a ship needs to pass, the traffic on the bridge stops, and the drawbridge is raised to let the ship pass through.

It took eight years to complete the construction of the Tower Bridge.

WONDERS OF THE WORLD

▶ The Ponte Vecchio, Florence, Italy

The Ponte Vecchio was built in 1345 over the Arno river, in Florence, Italy. The bridge is supported by two stone piers, shaped like the front of a boat. With big shopping stores built on it, the bridge is one of it's kind.

△ The Ponte Vecchio is Europe's oldest arch bridge.

FUN FACTS!

The Golden Gate bridge is made up of cables that are enough to encircle the earth, three times at the equator.

▽ The Seto Ohashi Bridge, Japan

Six bridges join the Honshu and the Shikoku islands in Japan. About 12.2 kms in length, this series of double-deck bridges have a separate track for electric trains as well. These bridges stretch over five small islands. One of the Seto Ohashi bridges, the Minami Bisan Seto, is the longest single bridge in the world.

▽ The Seto Ohashi Bridge is the world's longest two-tiered bridge.

Grand Monuments

Castles and forts were built by the kings in order to protect themselves from invasion. Since they were also home to the high and the mighty, they had to be attractive as well as strong. The architecture and the design of these castles varied, depending on the location and the requirement of the particular king. Some of them were strong enough to last several centuries.

❯ The Neuschwanstein Castle, Bavaria

King Ludwig II of Bavaria built this castle in the late 19th century. A very popular tourist attraction, this castle is made up of a number of tall towers, steep roofs and balconies. This makes it look like a typical medieval castle. Walt Disney's Enchanted Castle of Disneyland has been modelled on this castle.

⌃ *The Castle was designed by Christian Jank, who was also the king's personal artist.*

⌄ The Samurai Castle, Japan

The Himeji Castle is one of the most impressive of all samurai castles. It was built in the 14th century, when the warlords were the most powerful section of the society in Japan. They paid warriors, known as 'samurai', to fight for them. Hence, the name. This castle has five stories, and the walls have white plaster to protect the wooden frame from fire.

The Samurai castle was originally known as the Himeyama castle. ⌄

WONDERS OF THE WORLD

⌄ Masada fortress, Israel

A national symbol of Israel, the history of this mountain fortress is very grim. For two years, the Jews fighting the Romans, were trapped in this fortress. However, rather than surrendering or being captured, 959 out of the 966 people trapped, decided to kill themselves on 15th April, 73 AD. Since then, this fortress has become a symbol of honour for the people of Isreal.

The fortress of Masada was identified in the year 1842.

⟩ Statue of Liberty, U.S.A

The original torch of the Statue of Liberty was replaced in 1986.

This 302 feet tall statue, holding a torch in its hand, is the most famous symbol of freedom and democracy. Located on the 12-acre Liberty Island in New York Harbour, the Statue of Liberty was a gift of international friendship from the people of France to the people of the United States. Different pieces of the statue were shipped in 210 crates. Did you know that the seven spikes in the crown stand for the seven continents?

⌄ Victory Arch, Paris, France

Napoleon built the 'Arc de Triomphe' to celebrate his victory in the Battle of Austerlitz. Built in a Roman style, work on the arch commenced in 1806 and was completed in 1836. The arch has beautiful sculptures, adorning its walls.

⟨ *There is a small museum inside the Victory Arch.*

FUN FACTS!
The Sacsayhuaman fortress in Peru was built in 1520. The fortress was constructed with huge stones that were put together, without using any cement. Some of these stones weighed more than 100 tons!

Royal Palaces

In ancient days, palaces symbolised luxury and power. The more powerful the king, the more grandeur and affluence his palace displayed. Even today, palaces built in Saudi Arabia and Brunei can boast of opulence that is unparalleled. Kings also commemorated their victories or marked special events by building a monument or a memorial.

> Buckingham Palace, London

Home to the royal family of Britain and the Queen's official residence, the Buckingham palace was made in 1837. Queen Victoria was the first one to live there. It was originally owned by the Dukes of Buckingham, hence the name Buckingham. The Palace is open to visitors on a regular basis, and personifies elegance and style.

Nearly 400 people work at the Buckingham palace

⌄ The Palace of Versailles, France

This grand palace was built in the 1600s as a residence for the kings of France. It took 40 years for the palace to be completed. With 1300 rooms and gardens spread in about 50 acres of land, the palace is an architectural masterpiece.

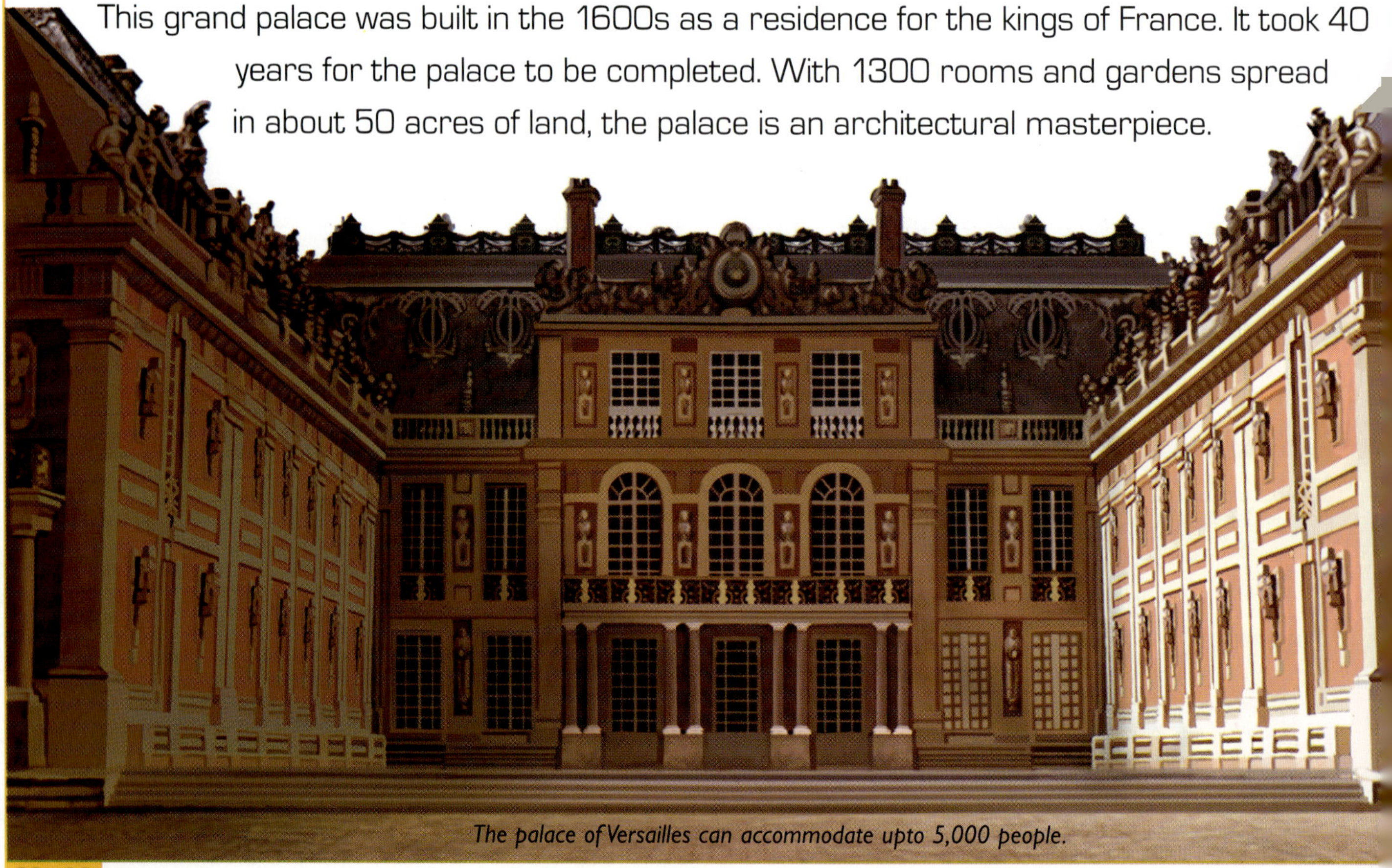

The palace of Versailles can accommodate upto 5,000 people.

WONDERS OF THE WORLD

Blenheim Palace, England

Built between 1705-25, this grand palace with elegant rooms and sprawling gardens was made as a gesture of gratitude by Queen Anne for the Duke of Marlborough, as he had pitched in a strong battle against the French, and had emerged victorious.

Winston Churchill was born in the Blenheim Palace.

Winter Palace, St. Petersburg, Russia

When Peter the Great became a tsar (ruler in Russian), he wanted to make a palace as grand as the palace of Versailles. Completed in 1762, this palace has 1500 rooms. It was called the Winter Palace and and was home to the Russian tsars till the Russian Revolution of 1917.

The Winter palace is located on the banks of the river Neva.

Imperial Palace, Beijing, China

Built within the Forbidden City, this magnificent palace was the home of Chinese emperors for nearly 500 years, until 1911. The palace is not open to the public. The only people who can enter the Forbidden City are the royal family members and their staff. The palace has 9000 rooms, and is surrounded by beautiful gardens and streams.

The Imperial Palace covers an area of 250 acres.

FUN FACTS!

According to the Guinness Book of Records, the grand palace of the Sultan of Brunei is the largest residence in the world. It has 1,788 rooms and 257 bathrooms.

Ancient Cities

Most of the earliest known human settlements existed either on the banks of a river or very close to it. It was the capital city that thrived more than the other cities since it was the seat of power. The capital also became the cultural and the economic hub. Over the centuries, most of the ancient cities have completely dissapeared, and what remains of them are just the ruins. These ruins convey a lot about the place and the age in which they existed. They also give us an idea about the lifestyle of its inhabitants, trade and commerce, and the social customs that were followed at that particular time.

Chang'an, China

Chang'an, meaning 'Perpetual Peace' also known as Xi'an, was the capital city of China during the reign of the Han dynasty. About 3,100 years old, the city was surrounded by a wall. The remains of the forts recall the grandeur of a bygone era. As the capital of 13 dynasties of Chinese emperors, it was one of the most important cities in ancient China.

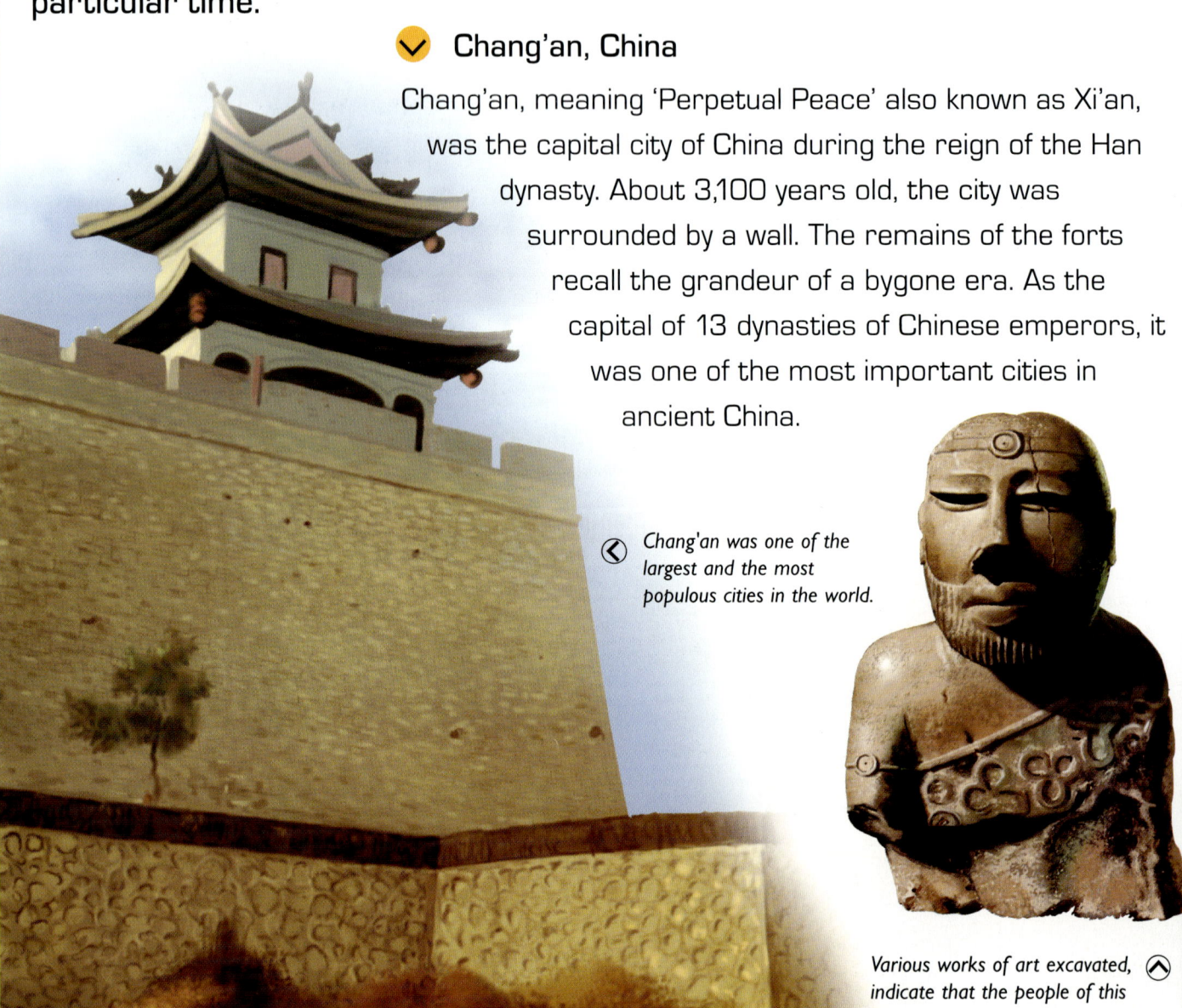

Chang'an was one of the largest and the most populous cities in the world.

Various works of art excavated, indicate that the people of this civilisation had fine artistic sensibilities.

WONDERS OF THE WORLD

> Mohenjo daro and Harappa

Located partly in Pakistan and partly in western India, the Indus Valley Civilisation thrived thousands of years ago. It was the largest of the four ancient civilisations – Egyptian, Mesopotamian, Indian and Chinese. The ruins of the city throw light on the meticulous city planning with straight streets, central baths, good water supply, and proper drainage and sewage system. Today, efforts are being made to protect the ruins from further damage.

⌃ *The people of Mohenjo daro and Harappa were the first to cultivate cotton for the production of cloth.*

⌄ Pompeii, Italy

The ruins of Pompeii were found near Naples in modern Italy. Pompeii was a thriving trade centre and a prosperous town before it was completely destroyed, when Mount Vesuvius erupted in 79 AD. The volcanic eruption buried the city under several feet of volcanic ash, and it was lost for almost 1,600 years, before it's ruins were discovered accidently. The excavation of the Pompeii ruins have thrown light on a city, which was a thriving centre of the Roman Empire. Today, it is one of Italy's leading tourist attractions and a UN World Heritage site.

⌄ *Nearly 20,000 people inhabited Pompeii at the time of the eruption.*

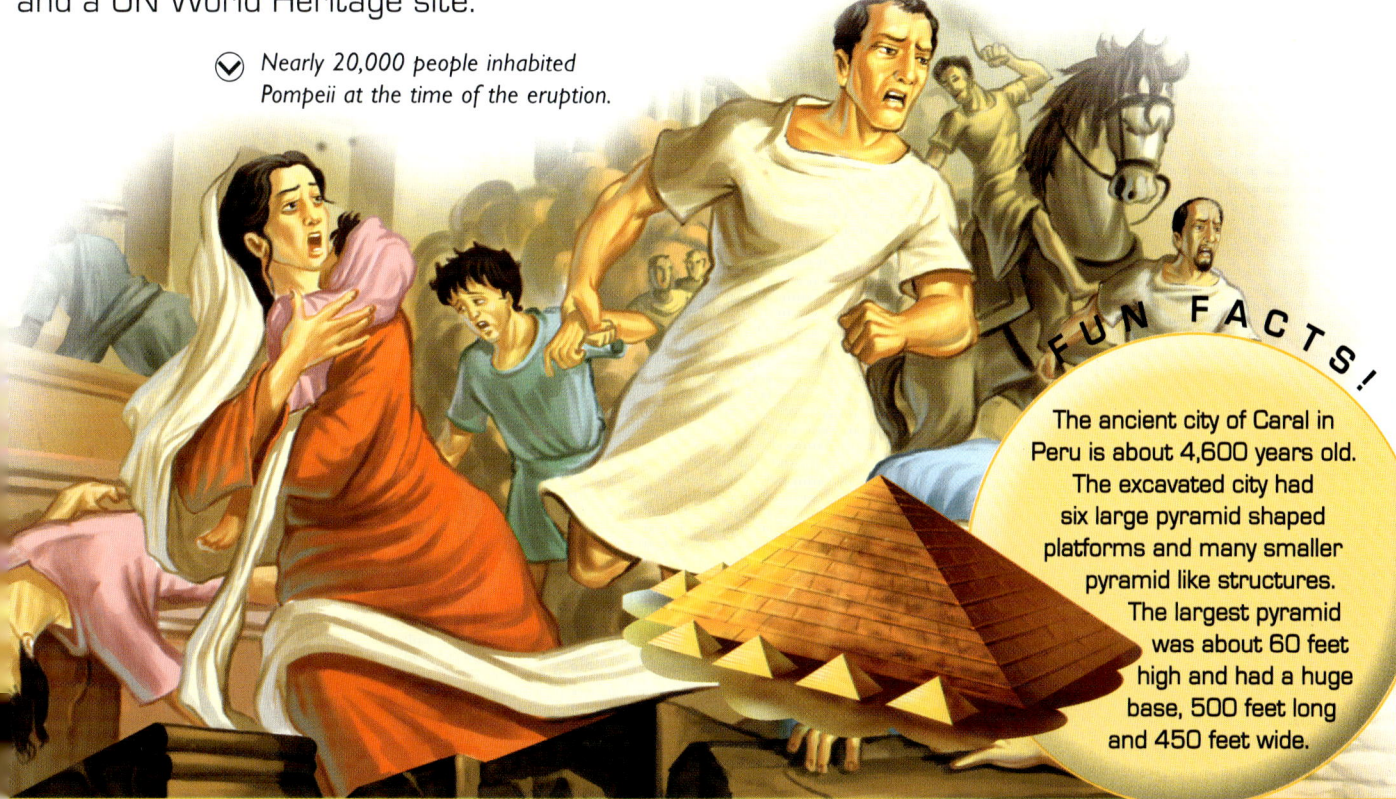

FUN FACTS!

The ancient city of Caral in Peru is about 4,600 years old. The excavated city had six large pyramid shaped platforms and many smaller pyramid like structures. The largest pyramid was about 60 feet high and had a huge base, 500 feet long and 450 feet wide.

The World's Tallest Buildings

In a bid to touch the skies, man designed skyscrapers. These new high-rise buildings are so tall that they almost seem to be defying the law of gravity!

> Sears Tower, Chicago, U.S.A

This is the tallest building in the United States, and the third tallest in the world. This 110-storey building has shops, offices and restaurants. It is a major tourist attraction. On a clear day, the Tower's Skydeck, which is situated on the 103rd floor, offers a wonderful view of four states – Illinois, Indiana, Michigan and Wisconsin.

< Taipei 101, Taiwan

Taipei 101, is a 101-floor skyscraper in Taipei city, Taiwan. It is the tallest building in the world and a new financial centre in Taipei. The building is a marvel of modern engineering.

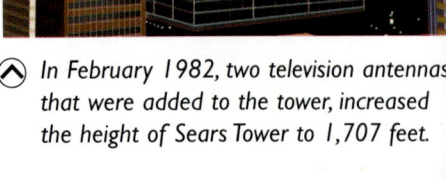
In February 1982, two television antennas that were added to the tower, increased the height of Sears Tower to 1,707 feet.

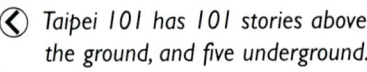
Taipei 101 has 101 stories above the ground, and five underground.

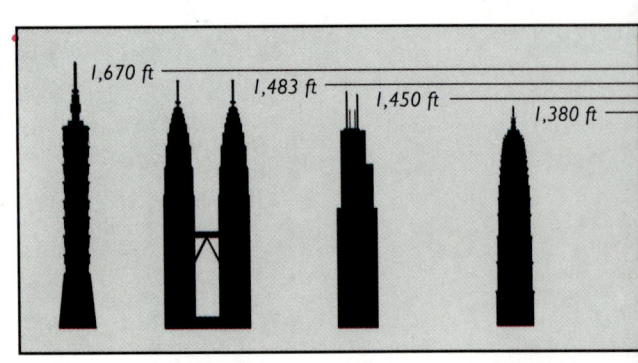

Taipei 101 Taipei	Petronas 1&2 Towers	Sears Tower Chicago	Jin Mao Building Shanghai
1,670 ft	1,483 ft	1,450 ft	1,380 ft

WONDERS OF THE WORLD

⌄ Petronas Towers, Kuala Lumpur, Malaysia

The Petronas Twin Towers are currently the tallest twin towers in the world. At a height of 1483 feet, the Petronas was the tallest building in the world until Taipei 101 took over as the tallest building on October 17, 2003.

› Jin Mao Building, Shanghai, China

The Jin Mao Building or the Jin Mao Tower in China is an 88 storey skyscraper. The building has several offices and the Shanghai Grand Hyatt hotel.

The Jin Mao Building reportedly has a daily maintenance cost of 1 million RMB or US$121,000. ›

‹ *Different construction companies were hired to build the Petronas Twin Towers, and they were made to compete against one another.*

FUN FACTS!

The twin Petronas Towers in Kuala Lumpur, Malaysia, have about 32,000 windows.

Holy Cities

Almost every religion of the world has certain spots that have religious significance. It could be due to a miraculous event occuring there or due to the birth of a holy person. Over time, believers have made shrines in the form of mosques, churches and temples. Pilgrims travel far and wide to visit these shrines to pray or show their reverence.

Santiago de Compostela, Spain

In the year 813 AD, a hermit saw a star, much like the star of Bethlehem, shining on a spot in a field. At that particular spot, he discovered a tomb, believed to be that of Saint James. When the king was told of this, he ordered a shrine that came to be known as 'Santiago de Compostela', to be built. He also named St James the patron saint of Spain.

The revered body of Saint James lies beneath the high altar in a silver coffer inside the cathedral.

Hindus believe that dying in Varanasi, guarantees freedom from the cycle of birth and rebirth.

Jerusalem

The holy city of Jerusalem is an ancient Middle Eastern city, and holds religious significance for the Jews, the Muslims and the Christians. It has a diverse and varied set of cultures, religions, nationalities and socio-economic groups. The section called the 'Old City' is surrounded by walls and has four quarters–Armenian, Muslims, Jews and Christians. The old city walls were built in the 16th century. The famous 'Dome of the Rock' shrine was built by the Muslims in 691 AD.

WONDERS OF THE WORLD

> ### Mecca, Saudi Arabia

Mecca, located about 80 km from the Red Sea, is the holiest site of Islam. Every year, Muslims from all over the world travel to Mecca for a pilgrimage known as the 'Haj'. They believe that this is the birthplace of Prophet Muhammad and the first place created on Earth.

> ### Varanasi, India

Located on the banks of the river Ganga, Varanasi is one of the holiest cities for the Hindus. People travel from all over the world to bathe in the holy waters of the Ganges and redeem themselves of all sins. The river bank is lined with several temples, dedicated to various Hindu gods and goddesses.

It is believed that the 'Kaaba' was built by Abraham.

FUN FACTS!

The city of Jerusalem contains more temples mosques and churches per square foot, than any other city in the world.

Sculptures and Memorials

Since times immemorial, sculptures and memorials have been built to mark an event or honour a god or a king.

The statue of Jesus was designed by the French-Polish architect Paul Landowsky.

The Statue of Jesus Christ, Brazil

Weighing over 1000 tonnes, this 98 feet statue of Jesus Christ is placed on the Corcovado mountain in the Tijuca Forest National Park, overlooking the city of Rio de Janeiro in Brazil, South America. It took five years to build this statue, and was completed in 1931 to mark the 100th year of Brazilian independence. It is so brightly lit at night that it can be seen clearly from anywhere in the city.

The Taj Mahal, India

The Taj Mahal was built by the Mughal emperor, Shah Jahan, in the memory of his wife, Mumtaz Mahal. Built in Agra, India, it is made of white marble. Semi-precious stones, intricate carvings, floral patterns and passages from the holy Quran, adorn the walls and the arches. The beautiful gardens, fountains and the minarets add to its mystique. After his death, Shah Jahan was also laid to rest by his queen's side. The Taj Mahal has always been associated with both, beauty and love.

The Taj Mahal was constructed by a workforce of approximately 20,000 people.

WONDERS OF THE WORLD

The Motherland, Russia

This 270 feet high statue of the Motherland is the largest concrete, full-figure statue in the world. It was made in 1967, and is located in Volgograd, Russia. The statue was built as a mark of respect to the brave Russians, who fought a battle at Stalingrad, in the Second World War. The statue depicts a mother standing guard over her country, her raised sword threatening to destroy her enemies, and calling on others to follow her example.

The statue of Motherland measures about 85 meters, from the tip of her sword to the top of the plinth.

The Statue of Peter the Great, St Petersburg, Russia

Commissioned by Catherine the Great, this striking statue is one of the finest monuments in St. Petersburg. It stands on Senate Square, facing the Neva River. This statue of Peter the Great on a horseback, has his horse stepping on a snake – perhaps representing the enemies of Russia.

Installed in 1782, the statue of Peter the Great, was built by the French sculptor Etienne Maurice Falconet.

FUN FACTS

The Trajan's Column in Rome is a 38 metre high marble monument made by emperor Trajan in 113 AD.

Temples, Mosques and Churches I

Shrines and temples have been built by humans since ancient times to honour the gods or conduct sacred rituals. Each faith has a special place of worship, distinguished by its architecture, location or the adornments used in it.

> St. Peter's Basilica, Rome

St. Peter's is located in the Vatican City, Rome. It was started in 349 AD.by emperor Constantine, the first Christian emperor of Rome. It was built on a spot where Saint Peter, the chief apostle of Jesus Christ, had been buried in 64 AD. However, it was only between 1506-1614, that active work to complete the church was undertaken. The basilica's dome, designed by Michelangelo, is the largest dome in the world, measuring 42 metre in diameter and is more than 450 feet high. The interior has 45 altars, and priceless artistic creations by famous artists such as Michelangelo, Bernini and Canova.

> *St Peter's is the largest church in the world and it can hold over 60,000 people.*

● The Great Hassan II Mosque, Morocco

Built in 1993 on the edge of the ocean, The Great Hassan II Mosque is shaped like a ship rising out of water. About 3,300 craftsmen worked hard to complete this mosque. It has the world's tallest minaret of any mosque (200 meters), and a retractable roof, which in three minutes can transform the prayer hall into a patio.

WONDERS OF THE WORLD

The Shah Faisal Mosque, Islamabad

The Shah Faisal Mosque near Islamabad, Pakistan, is the biggest mosque in the world. Built as a giant eight-faceted desert tent, the central hall is made of white marble and decorated with mosaics and a grand chandelier. It can accommodate upto 100,000 people in the prayer hall and the courtyard, and a further 200,000 in the adjacent grounds. The total area of the complex is 47 acres.

The Shah Faisal mosque was constructed in 1976 and was funded by the government of Saudi Arabia.

The Westminster Abbey, Britain

An architectural masterpiece, the Westminster Abbey has been the setting for every coronation since 1066. It is also the burial place of kings, statesmen, poets, scientists, warriors and musicians. It is used for both regular worship as well as for other royal occasions. In 1965-66, the Abbey celebrated its 900th anniversary.

Over three thousand people are buried at the Westminster Abbey.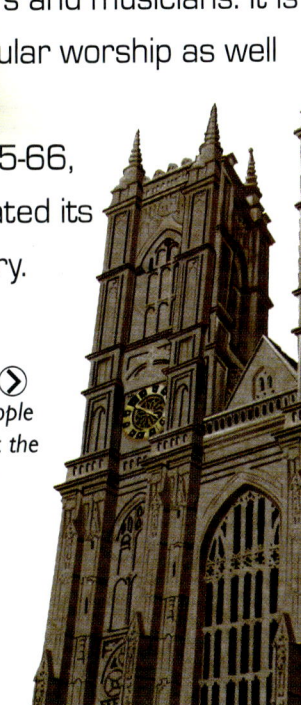

FUN FACTS!

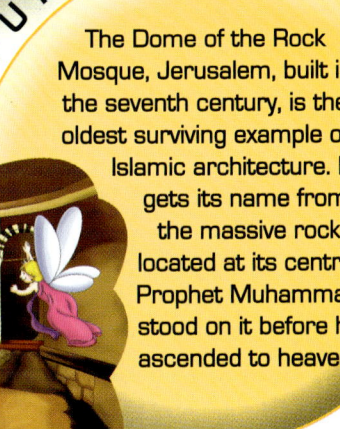

The Dome of the Rock Mosque, Jerusalem, built in the seventh century, is the oldest surviving example of Islamic architecture. It gets its name from the massive rock located at its centre. Prophet Muhammad stood on it before he ascended to heaven.

Temples, Mosques and Churches II

◀ The Chartres Cathedral, France

Started in 1194, the Chartres cathedral took about 450 years to be completed! Known for its stained glass windows, the cathedral is considered one of the finest examples of the 'Gothic' style of architecture in France.

▼ The Borobudur Temple, Java, Indonesia

The Borobudur temple in Indonesia was built by Sanmaratungga in the 8th century, and is the biggest Buddhist temple in the world. The temple was discovered in 1814 by Sir Thomas Stanford Raffles, in a ruined condition, buried under volcanic ash. The upper part of the temple has 72 bell-shaped structures called stupas. Each stupa is pierced by numerous decorative objects. Statues of the Buddha sit inside these enclosures.

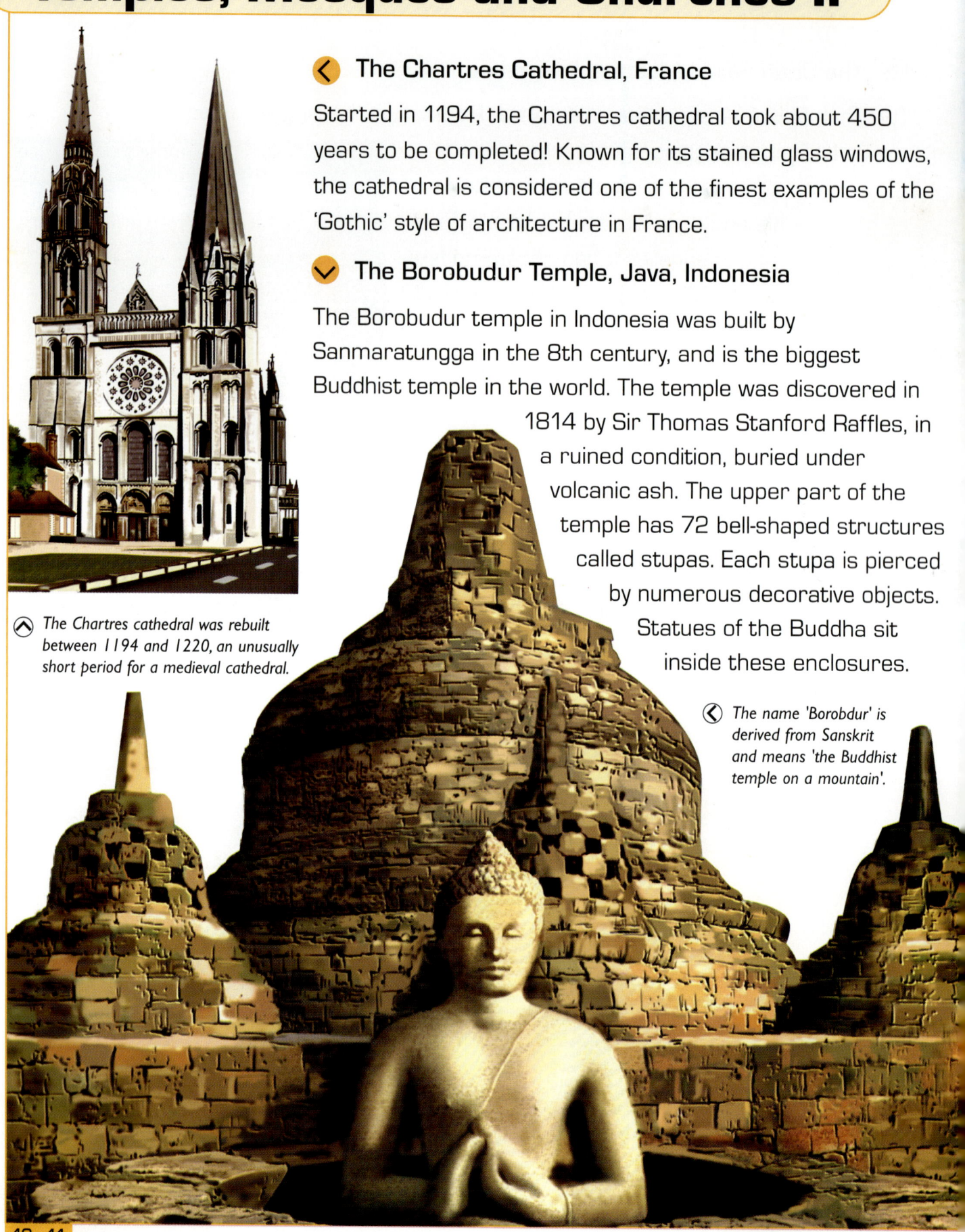

⌃ The Chartres cathedral was rebuilt between 1194 and 1220, an unusually short period for a medieval cathedral.

◀ The name 'Borobdur' is derived from Sanskrit and means 'the Buddhist temple on a mountain'.

WONDERS OF THE WORLD

The Sultan Ahmed Mosque is the only mosque in Turkey that has six minarets.

The Blue Mosque, Istanbul, Turkey

This mosque was built by Sultan Ahmed I in 1609 and took seven years to be completed. It is generally referred to as the 'Blue Mosque' because of the beautiful blue Iznik tiles, which make up its interiors. It has six minarets and the surrounding complex has a school, a tomb, a hospital, a caravanserai, a primary school, a public kitchen and a market.

The Golden Temple, Amritsar, India

Widely known as the Golden Temple, the Harimandir Sahib means the 'Temple of God', 'Hari' meaning god and 'Mandir' meaning temple. This temple, in the Indian state of Punjab, has been the religious place of worship for the Sikhs, since the 16th century. The temple has been renovated several times. When the roof was regilded in 1830, about 100 kgs of gold was used. An underground spring fills the lake that surrounds the temple.

The Harminder Sahib temple has four entrances, signifying, acceptance and openness.

FUN FACTS!

Lhasa is the capital of Tibet. It is considered to be a holy city because of the famous Potala Palace, which is home to the Dalai Lama, the religious head of the Tibetians.

World's Tallest, Highest, Longest, Largest

Nature bears some of the most wondorous sights. In terms of sheer size, these wonders not only inspire awe, but also reverence.

- **Longest Rivers**
  - Nile, Egypt (approx 4145 miles).
  - Amazon, Brazil (4007 miles)
  - Yangtze, China (3915 miles)
  - Mississipi-Missouri - Red Rock, U.S.A (3710 miles)
  - Yenisey - Angara-Selenga, Mongolia (3442 miles)

- **Highest Waterfalls**
  - Angel Falls, Venezuela
  - Tugela, South Africa
  - Utigard, Norway
  - Mongefossen, Norway
  - Yosemite, U.S

- **Highest Mountains**
  - Mount Everest, Asia
  - Acongcagua, South America
  - Mount McKinley, North America
  - Kilimanjaro, Africa
  - El'brus, Europe
  - Vinson Massif, Antarctica Mount Kosciusko, Australia

- **Largest continent**
  - Asia

- **Longest Suspension Bridge**
  - Alaska-Kaijkyo Bridge, Japan

- **Largest and Deepest Ocean**
  - Pacific Ocean

- **Largest country**
  - Russia

- **Largest Stadium**
  - Strahov Stadium, Prague

- **Largest Church**
  - Basilica of St. Peter, Vatican City

WONDERS OF THE WORLD

- **Largest Sea**
  - Coral Sea

- **Largest Delta**
  - Sunderbans (Ganga-Brahmaputra Delta)

- **Longest Railway Platform**
  - Kharagpur, West Bengal, India

- **Largest Desert**
  - Sahara, North Africa

- **Largest River**
  - Amazon, Brazil

- **Largest Freshwater Lake**
  - Lake Superior, Canada-USA

- **Largest Saltwater Lake**
  - Caspian Sea

Did you know?

1. How many ancient wonders were listed down by Philo?
2. What is another name for a ruler in Russia?
3. Which church later became a mosque?
4. How many years did it take for the Taj Mahal in India to be completed?
5. Which country gifted the Statue of Liberty to America?
6. What were Japanese warriors called?
7. Which mountain carving links the faces of four great Presidents of America?
8. Name the longest undersea tunnel in the world.
9. Where is the "Old Faithful" geyser located?
10. Which is the highest building in the world?

WONDERS OF THE WORLD

11. Who were the first people to summit the Mount Everest?
12. What is the electric power, made from the force of water called?
13. What is the name of the palace, which is the official home of the British royal family?
14. On which river is the Tower Bridge of England built?
15. Which is the world's biggest canyon?
16. Where is the Gateway to the West located?
17. Where is the world's biggest mosque located?
18. Where can you see the Moai Statues?
19. Where is the statue of Peter the Great located?
20. Which is the only ancient wonder that has survived?

Answers

1. Seven
2. Tsar
3. The church of Hagia Sophia in Constantinople
4. 22 years
5. France
6. Samurai
7. Mount Rushmore National Memorial
8. Channel Tunnel
9. Yellowstone National Park, U.S.A
10. Taipei 101, Taiwan
11. Edmund Hillary and Tenzing Norgay
12. Hydroelectricity
13. Buckingham Palace
14. River Thames
15. The Grand Canyon, U.S.A
16. St. Louis, Missouri, U.S.A
17. Pakistan
18. Easter Island
19. St. Petersburg, Russia
20. The Great Pyramid of Giza